Safety on the School Bus

Sarah Florence

Rosen REAL READERS

I0809723

The Rosen Publishing Group, Inc.
New York

I go to school on the school bus.

Billy and I sit down.

We follow the rules.

We listen to the bus driver.

We stay in our seats.

The bus stops. We stand up and go to school.

Words to Know

bus driver

school bus

seat